Though I Walk ...

DIVINE RESCUE FROM THE VALLEY

Even though I walk through the valley of the shadow of death, I will fear no evil, for you are with me; your rod and your staff, they comfort me.
Psalm 23:4

COMPILED BY:

PASTOR MARILYN E. PORTER

Though I Walk...

DIVINE RESCUE FROM THE VALLEY

Foreword by
Angela R. Edwards

Pastor Marilyn E. Porter

Soulidified Publishing LLC™, Atlanta, GA

a Subsidiary of Pearly Gates Publishing LLC™

Though I Walk...
Divine Rescue From the Valley

ISBN 13: 978-1945117534
ISBN 10: 1945117532

Published by:
Soulidified Publishing LLC™,
a Christian Publisher located in
Atlanta, Georgia (USA)

Foreword
By Angela R. Edwards

I want to *first* give glory and honor to God for this amazing opportunity to work alongside Pastor Marilyn E. Porter and the other four Women of God (WOG) who came together to perfectly knit this project for God's daughters.

Pastor Marilyn E. Porter's God-inspired visions **never** cease to amaze me! I can recall a time not too long ago when she held a video conference where she expertly broke down the 23rd Psalm into "plain speak". She made it **SO** plain, I never read that particular Psalm of David the same ever since.

Though I Walk...Divine Rescue From the Valley is definitely an extension of that teaching. Just as God always does for divine assignments, he brought together women whose stories of **"going through"** share one common theme: **God kept them.** Kept them from what, you ask?

I would love to sit here and say, "*Oh, He kept them from pain, heartache, depression, thoughts of suicide, promiscuity, and off of the brinks of death*" - but I can't.

I **will** tell you that God brought them through for a time such as this.

I **will** tell you that **God** - *Elohim: The All-Powerful One*; **God** - *Jehovah-Rapha: The Lord Who Heals*; and **God** - *Jehovah-Rohi: The Lord My Shepherd* brought forth healing of the heart, mind, and soul of each of the ladies who contributed their truths penned on these pages.

I, too, have had valley experiences (*who hasn't*): **BUT GOD!** I found myself relating on multiple levels to each and every single story shared here. These WOG lay it all out there for you. There's no shame. There's no holding a little bit back so as to not offend anyone. *No.* What's penned on these pages is meant to be, and God knows there is something here that **YOU** need.

Whatever your valley experience entails, rest assured: **You are not alone.** Scripture tells us there is *NOTHING* new under the sun (Ecclesiastes 1:9). With that being said, you can know that should you be a victim of molestation and are *still* processing the pain some 10, 20, 30 or more years later, **there is hope in Christ Jesus!** You can know that when the doctor's report said that there's nothing more he can do, **there is hope in Christ Jesus!** You can know that when your body is dying from the inside out and you can't seem to understand the "why", **there is hope in Christ Jesus!** You can know that when you attempted suicide and were unsuccessful, **there is hope in Christ Jesus!**

I digress. These are not "*just stories*"...they are **TESTIMONIES** of God's goodness, grace, and mercy. These women did nothing extraordinary to earn God's protection. As a matter-of-fact, they will openly share their sinful nature and how God rescued them in spite of. Today, these same women will attest to being covered by undeserved grace.

GLORY TO GOD!

It takes a certain level of boldness and surety in your Christian walk to *openly* share 'your ugliness' with the world. These women have both, as proven evident in the fact that their names are attached to their individual testimonies. I, for one, thank God for them. I am **further** encouraged and strengthened in my own walk through the reading of their truths.

It is my sincere prayer that though **YOU** *will* walk through the valley, your divine rescue will come. Never stop believing God will do just what He says He will do in His Word.

I leave you with this passage of Scripture taken from GOD'S WORD Translation™:

"God is not like people. He tells no lies. He is not like humans. He doesn't change his mind. When He says something, He does it. When He makes a promise, He keeps it" (Numbers 23:19).

Walk your walk through the valley - and fear **NO** evil, for God is with you always.

God bless!

~ Angela R. Edwards
Presenter & Biblical Adviser, Motivational Outreach Ministers and Mentors
Longtime Friend and Colleague

PSALM 23
GOD'S WORD Translation™

1. The Lord is my shepherd.
I am never in need.

2. He makes me lie down in green pastures.
He leads me beside peaceful waters.

3. He renews my soul.
He guides me along the paths of righteousness
for the sake of His name.

**4. *Even though I walk through the dark valley of death,
because you are with me, I fear no harm.
Your rod and your staff give me courage.***

5. You prepare a banquet for me while my enemies watch.
You anoint my head with oil.
My cup overflows.

6. Certainly, goodness and mercy will stay close to me all the
days of my life, and I will remain in the Lord's house for days
without end.

Introduction

Beloved,

When God speaks, you **must** listen.

I was instructed to compile stories from people of God who were "social proof" - *if you will* - of the goodness of God. I was **further** instructed to do so modeling the 23rd Psalm.

Though I Walk... is the first in a series, and I am super-excited to witness how this book blesses all those who read it.

Keep your eyes open for book number two, *By the Still Waters...*

~ Dr. M.E. Porter

Table of Contents

Minister Andrea Spencer, the Associate Minister of the *Word 4 H.E.R. Ministry*, was licensed on September 18, 2016 by Pastor David Cross of the Liberty Church in Gardena, California. She accepted the call to ministry in 2003. Since that time, she has ministered to abused and hurting women. Minister Spencer is a 47-year survivor of sexual assault and is a Certified Sexual Assault Advocate with the YWCA. She was born in St. Louis, Missouri and raised in Meridian, Mississippi. She is married to Minister Tommy Spencer and has one adult son. Andrea is a member of Zeta Phi Beta Sorority, Inc.

Ministry: The Word 4 H.E.R (Healed, Empowered, Restored)

Dedication

My story is dedicated to hurting and abused women everywhere.

Acknowledgment

To my *Word 4 H.E.R.* sisters.

Social Media:
Facebook (Andrea Harvey-Spencer)

Website:
www.TheWord4HER.com

Walking Through the Wilderness
By Minister Andrea Spencer

August 11, 1968.

That was a day I will *never* forget.

As I ran back into the house, I saw my father lying there bleeding to death. I began crying and screaming. My mother grabbed me and rushed me down the street to my Godmother's house. I stood on her porch - watching and wondering what happened. I was in disbelief as I watched them bring my father's lifeless body out of our home on a stretcher.

The tears began falling again. The one person I knew who *truly* loved me was gone...never to be seen again. That night, I cried myself to sleep, all the while wishing it was all a dream.

When I reflect back on the events of that day, I can truly say **God** protected me...

After returning home from church on that dreadful day, I witnessed my father and maternal grandfather drinking alcohol in the front yard with some of the men from the neighborhood. That was not an unusual sight because that is what they did on the weekend. What *was* unusual was the argument that erupted that spurred my father's anger. He left his company outside, entered the house, and began having words with my mother.

My grandfather, hearing the commotion, came to the door with one of his many guns and asked my father to stop. Well, that caused my father's anger to rise even more. He made his way to my grandfather's room and grabbed a rifle. A gun battle erupted. My mother *immediately* sat us children down on the floor and would not allow us to move so that we would stay out of harm's way. When the two men moved from the front of the house to the back, my mother rushed us outside.

God did not allow the bullets to come near us. Yes: **God** spared my life that day. I was 11 years old at the time.

After my father's death, I began feeling like my world had come to an end. I was a 'daddy's girl' and wanted so much to walk down the streets with him again as he played with my hair. There was a growing emptiness inside of me. I wanted so badly to be loved again.

One day, my mother went into the hospital to have a biopsy performed. As I walked to the hospital to visit her, I encountered one of the neighborhood boys who I knew - but didn't really *"know"*. He asked if he could walk with me. I replied, *"Yes!"* As we walked, I decided to take the long route to the hospital. We walked and talked all along the way. *I enjoyed his company...and the attention.*

As we approached one of the other hospitals near where my mother was, there was some construction taking place. I didn't give it much thought at the time...and I had **no** idea what was in store for me.

As the boy and I approached the under-construction hospital, he grabbed me by the arm and pulled me under the building. Once there, he threw me down to the ground, forced my legs open, and pushed my underwear to the side. I kicked and scratched him, but I couldn't scream. He wouldn't allow me to. Once he penetrated me, the kicking soon ceased and my body began to respond. As he was approaching his climax, he simply got up and left me there.

I pulled myself together and went on to see my mother in the hospital. I did not tell her what had just happened to me. *I didn't understand at the time that I was raped.* I didn't tell anyone about the incident - fearing I would get in trouble for letting him walk with me in the first place.

When I arrived home, I went straight to the bathroom and attempted to wash away the memories of the attack. I remember thinking, "*If my father was alive, that would not have happened*".

As I reflect back on that night, I now realize that God was with me - even during the attack. He did not allow that 14-year-old boy to leave me dead under that building. There was no one - *not a single person* - around to see him. He could have **easily** left me there...lifeless - **but God!**

After that attack, I began to think about the initial feeling of the sexual encounter after he penetrated me. I wanted to feel that feeling again. I began trying to use various objects to see if I could obtain that exact feeling *(I was too young to know anything about vibrators and other sex toys)*. All the while, my interest in boys grew - and the battle with the mind began.

I was in 7th grade when I was raped. By the time high school graduation came, I was **very** promiscuous.

My father's death and the rape led me to live a life of sadness, guilt, shame, insecurity, abandonment, low self-esteem, and many other internalized issues. It is **only** because of God's grace and mercy that I am able to sit here and write this story.

I have endured so many heartaches and pains. I had many failed relationships - each one a futile attempt to fill the void left by my father's death. *I cannot begin to tell you the number of men I had sex with.* I **can** tell you sex does **not** bring you love; it brings you even **more** heartache and **more** pain.

In 1979, I married my first husband. It was not the happiest time in my life because the void that was left by my father's death was still there. The marriage ended in divorce in 1988. The loneliness returned. I found myself "wandering around in the wilderness" again - *still* making attempts to fill that void.

In 1990, a transformation began to take place in my life. God began to reveal what I was missing.

I was attending church in Compton, California at the time. Every Sunday (without fail), I approached the altar and asked God to fill me with His Holy Spirit - not really knowing what I was asking for.

I was working part-time for the U.S. Census Bureau and was tasked with going door to door enumerating the households. I visited **many** Christian homes and began to hunger to know more about the Word of God. I met a man of God who began to minister God's Word to me. (*Mind you: I had been attending church since the age of eight, but I did not* **know** *the Word of God.*) The more I began to seek God and His Word, the more He revealed Himself to me. I soon became filled with the Holy Spirit with the evidence of speaking in tongues.

That was the turning point in my life.

I grew closer to the Lord and began attending a church where I could learn more of God's Word. Although I was in a Word-teaching church, the void to be loved still needed to be filled. I was determined to do things *God's* way, and because of that, I met and married my second husband after only five months of dating.

Well, shortly after we married, things began to go downhill. After four years of marriage, I found myself filing for divorce...again. A year later, I married my third husband; a substance-abuser. That was a **very** rough ride for me because I had never dealt with a man who used drugs. We were separated more than we were together due to his drug use. After four years of dealing with his visits to recovery homes and numerous hospital stays, I decided to call it quits. That was in 1998.

If I don't know anything else, one thing I do know is that God was with me - in spite of my disobedience.

In 1999, I returned to college to obtain my Masters of Arts Degree, which was accomplished in December 2000. Prior to obtaining my degree, I met my fourth husband.

NOTE: It doesn't pay to ignore the warning signs!

In 2002, we married. In 2006, he moved out of our home and into that of another woman. That was probably the biggest heartache of my life (*next to my dad's passing*) because I truly believed our relationship was fine. **I never saw it coming.** He filed for divorce - and even tried to sue *ME* for spousal support! After receiving the divorce papers, God used a co-worker to direct me to a divorce attorney who allowed me to make payments because I didn't have any money saved. When the divorce was final, I was left to pay off some credit card bills I had created - *but no spousal support for him!*

I wish I could say I learned my lesson after that, but I can't. Although I had been in the Word for almost 15 years, that void **still** existed. I found myself drifting back into a promiscuous lifestyle. I became angry with God and began pulling away from Him. God wouldn't let go of me, though! After wrestling back and forth with wanting to do things my way, I finally said, "*Okay, God: It is you and me until you decide to send me the one you have for me.*" I allowed God to fill the void and you know what I discovered? His love for me!

After surrendering to God and His will, the husband **GOD** had ordained for me quickly manifested. I had known my fifth husband for over 25 years. I would have never thought *he* was the man God had for me. So, after six years of waiting, slipping, falling, and doing things my way, God provided.

Once I found a place of contentment, God was able to move.

God allowed me to relocate from the state of Mississippi and live in Guam for two years. To date, I have resided in California for 34 years. After 40 years of wandering in the wilderness, at the age of 52, I was allowed to see the perpetrator who raped me **and** had the opportunity to tell him I forgive him.

God has done some great and awesome things in my life. I am now a Licensed Minister of the Gospel, sharing my testimony with hurting and abused women.

In September 2016, I turned 60 years old. I can truly say God has been with me every step of the way. He has allowed me to marry a Licensed and Ordained Minister of the Gospel - and we worship and serve the Lord *together*.

2 Corinthians 1:3-6 is a Scripture I hold dear to my heart because it is through the suffering that I have endured. It is through the suffering that I have been able to help others make it through.

God did not allow me to be killed.

God did not allow me to lose my mind and be institutionalized.

God was with me **all** the time.

"To God be the glory for the things that He has done!"

Evangelist Shante Burris is the Senior Ministry Assistant for *The Word 4 H.E.R.* Ministry. She is the youngest of eight children who was brought up in church and accepted Jesus as her Lord and Savior at the age of 12. She loves the Lord and has faithfully served Him in various ministry positions. Evangelist Burris accepted her call to Armor Bearer in 2005. She received her Bachelor of Science Degree in Business Administration in 2014.

Ministry: The Word 4 H.E.R (Healed, Empowered, Restored)

Dedication:

To my mother, Jacqueline, who is in Heaven, and my daughter, Kyarah, who always inspires me.

Acknowledgment:

To BIOGM, The Word 4 H.E.R. Ministry, and to Genae for always pushing me daily.

Website:

www.TheWord4HER.com

From Then to Now
By Evangelist Shante Burris

It's funny how the mind works. There are things that can be recalled from long ago that seem as if they just happened 'yesterday'. Then, there are moments in time that happened not so long ago, and they seem as if *years* have passed since transpiring. There are also occurrences that come along that you wish you could forget, yet they are always there...stored in your memory like a keepsake item to be held onto forever.

I have memories going as far back as going to Headstart. My favorite teacher's name was Iris Petite. She and my mom were the best of friends. Outside of school, the would enjoy hanging out with each other going to concerts and things of that nature.

We lived on 59th Street in Los Angeles, California. My aunt and her family lived a few doors down, and a cousin and her family lived across the street. Memories of my time on that block have faded over time; however, I do remember between the ages of four and five, **all** of us moved from 59th to 94th Street. Growing up there, we had no real need for 'outside friends' because there were so many of us around the same age living in the same house. We didn't need *anyone* to come over to play!

Let me back up for *just* a minute.

I am the youngest of eight: five boys and three girls. My mom would often tell me I was "the last of the Mohicans". When we moved from 59th Street, we moved in with my grandmother, aunt, **and** my aunt's three children. Needless to say: *We were a FULL house.*

I attended Manhattan Place Elementary from Kindergarten through 6th grade. My 6th grade class was the last to attend that particular elementary school because come the following year, 6th-graders would start attending middle school.

Growing up in a house full of children, you learn quickly who is the favorite...and who isn't. Me? I wasn't the favorite on **anyone's** list. As a child, I was rather clumsy. That didn't go over well with certain people. I was talked about because I was the darkest one in the family, had the shortest hair, and was "the ugliest". I even had one aunt who told me she didn't like me simply because I was born - *a girl!*

Life changed for me in a dramatic way when we moved, and while many of the memories of the time spent on 59th Street are almost nonexistent, there is one thing I can state with certainty: **I was a happy child, and in a moment - in the twinkling of an eye - *all* of that changed.**

I never really knew why we moved...although I have always wondered. I never asked. I rationalized it out: *We moved, so there had to be a good reason why.* For my young mind, that was good enough for me!

Looking back now, as I write my story, my tough times seem to have outweighed the good - but I would not change a thing I went through then nor any of the things I experienced since. **Everything** I have endured from childhood to present day has had a profound influence on my life and helped shape me into the person I am today.

When I was around eight years old, I was raped by one of my brothers. Out of **all** of my brothers, he was my *favorite*. He was the one I spent the most time with hanging out. Around that same age, I was also forced to perform oral sex on a few of the *female* members in our family. Other than sharing this information a few years ago with my best friend, I have never spoken about the sexual assault and abuse. No one in my family knew what happened to me. I had convinced myself that my nephew (*who was also going through his own issues with the family*) and I were against the world. I just **knew** there was no way a loving God would have allowed us to go through those things and not provide us a way out. My nephew and I did virtually everything together - and when we weren't together, I spent a lot of time outdoors (like most kids). When I was in the house, I would be in my room - *when I could find time to be in there alone* - praying to God and asking Him to remove me from the **Hell** I was in.

Some may wonder where my father was while all of the abuse was going on. Well, the answer is this: **He was doing whatever he wanted to do!** He was living his life without a worry in the world. Taking care of his child was not a high priority on his list. Now, that is not to say he *never* did a thing for me; rather, **everything** that needed to be done was handled by my grandmother - which was just fine with *her* because she was a control freak. Grandmother wanted to be in control of everything in his life from who he dated to how much money he could give me - **and** she decided the purpose the money was provided!

At the tender age of 10, I became an alcoholic. I could not function if I did not have a drink. That phase lasted eight years...until right after high school graduation.

Graduation night, I was at a pajama party at a hotel. There was every kind of liquor available that you could imagine, from *E&J* to *Night Train* and **everything** in between. Taking notice that the number of guys at the party far outnumbered the girls, I limited my alcohol consumption. I didn't want to get to the point where I didn't know what was going on around me or who was doing "what" to me. Even with that precaution in place, I was *still* attacked by one of the guys at the party. We were in the hotel room and someone turned the lights off. With the music blaring, no one heard my screams. I fought him off as much as I could and prayed that someone would come in before he raped me. **God heard my prayer.** Right before the guy had me completely pinned down, someone burst through the door. I was able to get away. I vowed from that moment on I would never drink again - and I haven't.

Moving forward to my young adult years...

Because of my predisposition when it came to sex, I really didn't have **any** boundaries when it came to intimacy. Keeping it honest: I became a whore. Whenever I wanted to have sex, I did - with no regard for who I was having sex with. It didn't matter to me if there was someone who was going to be hurt as a result. *Initially*, that was not a problem...until I started to attract the attention of married men.

The first married man I slept with was a complete surprise. I didn't find out he was married until after we had been together for a while. I ended that relationship, but the seed had already been planted. From that point forward, married men were all that appealed to me. *The funny thing here is that I would find myself ridiculing and talking down about women who entered into relationships with men who were married.* **NEVER** in my life did I envision being an early-20s female in those types of situations.

"You should not be so quick to pass judgment on people until you have walked a mile in their shoes", they say.

Ain't THAT the truth!

The married man I was involved with proved to be the life-altering one. He was the husband of a friend of mine, and when she found out about the affair, not only did it ruin her marriage and our friendship; both her household **and** mine were greatly affected. With all that I had endured while growing up, I had not experienced pain as immense as in that moment. The emotional and mental toll it took on me was damn near unbearable.

In the days-turned-months that passed, I was numb and had vowed - *as God was my witness* - to **never** even **speak** to another married man as long as I lived. I saw firsthand the trauma it caused. I felt bad for all the times I had spoken ill about other women who were in similar situations. While it may have been easy to get into that relationship, it was *very* difficult to get out of.

Since then, I have recommitted myself to the Lord and study His Word. I have had one other relationship since then and was blessed with a beautiful child. The relationship didn't last long - and (*in case you're wondering*) no; the guy was **not** married.

Today, my focus is on becoming the woman God intended for me to become and raising my daughter in a God-fearing home. I am patiently waiting for God to send the man I am to be with for the rest of my life. No longer will I operate *"in my feelings in the heat of the moment"*, **especially** since we are now living in a time when it seems customary that men not wear their wedding bands. I am not willing to go down *THAT* road again. I will wait on the Lord to send me my Boaz.

With all that I have gone through, no matter how bad the situation, I would not change a single thing that I have experienced. **All** of the trials, tribulations, ups, downs, the good, and the bad have shaped me into who I am today.

Remember the aunt I mentioned who told me she didn't like me because I was born a girl? Well, she had taken ill and was in the hospital for a few days. My mom and I went to visit her and, during the visit, she asked me if I knew why she was always so hard on me. I told her *"No"*. She proceeded to tell me that when I was younger (maybe around age three or four), I peed on her floor. When she told me to look at what I had done, I turned to her and said, *"So?"* She said at that moment, she knew I was tough and would be okay in life - no matter what might come my way. She added she knew **then** that I was strong and a survivor. At that moment, I knew I was loved by her. Any hard feelings I had been harboring toward her were *immediately* dismissed.

There are things that I (*like everyone walking this Earth*) still have to go through and deal with. Life is going to happen whether we want it to or not.

One thing I am still processing is the loss of my mother in 2014. I never thought I would have to say 'good-bye' to her so soon, but I thank God I was able to be with her and have the time to say *"Good-bye, Mom"*, knowing that **my** face was the last she saw before taking her final breath. That gives me some peace in knowing she didn't leave this earthly life alone with no one by her side.

My mother raised me to be strong and very independent. I am now in that mother-role. I have a six-year-old daughter to provide and care for. I am making sure she is brought up in the manner the Lord would have her be raised. I have to make sure the decisions I make are ones that are beneficial to her wellbeing and growth.

As adults, we always hear, *"Be careful about the things you do and say around children because they see and hear everything you do and say!"* While we know that to be factual, we **still** don't pay close enough attention until we have children of our own and see how our words and actions are repeated through them - and sometimes not in a positive way.

Knowing that, I have to be more mindful of the things I say and how I act or react to any given situation. I am, after all, raising up the next generation. In spite of the fact that there are and will be things my daughter will face as she matures, I have to ensure the strength, values, morals, and beliefs my own mother instilled in me will, in turn, be instilled in her. Doing so will enable her to face her trials while standing firm on her beliefs in God - and herself. I pray she will **never** compromise who she is to satisfy another or try to become a person others *try* to shape her to be.

Oftentimes, when we look at our lives and that of those around us, we tend to ask the hard questions: *"Why me? What did I do to be the one chosen to endure such pain and heartache? When will the problems (whatever they may be) end? Will I ever be happy?"* Well, I am here to give you the answers to those questions...the answers as I have come to realize and accept them.

GOD chose us to go through the pain because there is a work that only we can do. In order to be able to do the work and minister to the people, He will bring to us the following knowledge: *We have to understand the hurt, pain, and struggle others are now faced with.*

Know and understand this: In most cases, we did nothing to "deserve it". The simple answer is we were chosen and, as followers of Christ, we have to be able to identify with our Heavenly Father. We will **never** experience the pain He endured on the cross, but we, too, *will* suffer. Yes, the problems will end when everything the Lord set out for us to do is accomplished. We will be joyful when we are called Home (*Heaven*) for all eternity!

As I continue to live each day, I learn something new to help me get closer to where I am supposed to be in life. I may not be there yet, but I am not where I used to be! As I look back over my life, I am thankful to have made it this far.

Negativity can bring you down - if you let it. I, however, am living proof that **anyone** can change and do so for the better...in spite of the past.

Whenever I feel down or defeated, I just think of one specific passage of Scripture to give me strength:

"I can do all things through Christ who strengthens me"
(Philippians 4:13).

I am a survivor.

Genae "*The Destiny Designer*" Kulah is an ordained Prophetic Minister, Founder of *The Word 4 H.E.R.* (Healed, Empowered, and Restored) Ministry, Empowerment Coach, and Best-Selling Author. She received her Bachelor of Science Degree in Biblical Studies and Business Administration, as well as certification as a Church and Discipleship Consultant. Prophetess Kulah is also an Ambassador with the Pink Pulpit Crusade under the direction of Apostle Dr. Marilyn Porter.

Dedication

My story is dedicated to hurting and abused women everywhere.

Acknowledgment

To my Word 4 H.E.R. Sisters.

Social Media

YouTube: The Word 4 H.E.R.
Periscope: The Word 4 H.E.R.

Web: www.TheWord4Her.com

How She Became H.E.R. Story
By Prophetess Genae Kulah

My life began on June 16, 1971. I was born to Alfred Akki and Loretta Kulah - a 6 lb., 4 oz. baby with an attitude…according to the picture the hospital took of me.

Of course, I do not remember too much of my early years, but one thing I **do** recall with ease is the day I met Jesus. It was a warm, sunny day. My mom decided to take me to the park to play. As an only child, it was hard for me to make friends because I grew to love the solitude, but my mom felt that was unhealthy - so off I went to play. I met a few kids, but ultimately ended up alone…*just the way I liked it.* On the way home that particular day, she met a traveling evangelist who told her about his ministry. At the time, my mom was a practicing Catholic, so she didn't **really** pay much attention to that man - until later on that same night.

After arriving home, I ran my bath water and proceeded to enjoy the time in my homemade pool. Something caused me extreme fright while in the bathroom. I jumped out of the water and ran to my mother. She began praying and started to call the Catholic priest, but something made her hang up and call the evangelist instead. *I suppose he told her to come to his house because within an hour, that's where we were.*

He was a nice man with a wonderful wife and two daughters. He prayed with my mom. Then, he prayed with both of us. I do not know exactly *how,* but I understood what he was saying about believing in Jesus Christ and accepting Him as my personal Savior. I knew then I had a friend. I was so happy to have Jesus. I have no doubt I would not have survived what happened to me next **without** His presence.

It did not take long for my mom to dive in to learn the Holy Bible. She was always studying something, and she was given something she could study that would change her life. She went to **every** conference, Bible study, prayer meeting, and deliverance service she thought would help deepen her relationship with the Lord. I was her traveling buddy and enjoyed every second of it. I learned as much as my little mind was able to comprehend. Still, there are some things in life that are incomprehensible - especially at a young age.

Approximately a year after we began the faith journey, one of the men in my mother's Bible study class decided he wanted to be "closer" to me. *My mom had no idea just how close.* While she was preaching and teaching the Gospel, **that man** was teaching me things that only a woman should know.

Oh. Did I forget to mention? *I was only seven years old.*

The molestation by that evangelist led to others in the church violating me in ways **no** child should ever endure, especially "*in the name of the Lord*"! **How could that be the way God wanted me to feel love?** The molestation went on for five years. I had lost my identity through the turmoil. The only things that kept me sane were my love for music and my ability to write songs. I had so many songs that expressed my pain. I would sing them to God - *and Him only.* The demon of depression soon set in, and I tried to commit suicide.

The **first** try was at the age of 10.

I was tired of the pain. I was tired of feeling dirty. I was just plain, old **TIRED**. I swallowed some of my mother's pills and laid down, waiting for them to do their job and silence the hurt once and for all. I wanted the pain to stop…but it didn't. God would not allow me to die that way, so I continued to suffer in silence.

*I often wondered why those who said they loved and talked to God could not see the pain in **my** eyes.*

When I was finally able to tell my mom about the molestation, she acted on my behalf quickly. The evangelist who abused me for the *longest* amount of time made the **stupid** mistake of coming over when my mother called. After she confronted him, the police politely escorted him out of my life. Unfortunately, the damage was already done - but it wasn't *over*.

Once the church leaders found out about the accusations of molestation, they blamed my **mother** - instead of the pedophile. They even told the children in the church. I was labeled a whore and became very popular with the boys in the church…and very unpopular with the girls.

No one provided comfort to my mother nor me, which drove her into a deep depression. Therein began my up-and-down journey with mental illness.

My mom was diagnosed with a Manic-Depressive Disorder. Because of her condition, she was not able to adequately care for herself, so I had to do it for her. She would be in and out of the hospital often, which left me to fend for myself. I recall a time when I woke up and the front door was wide open. My mom had disappeared through that open door and did not return until the following morning. When I asked her where she had been, she could not tell me. I made the decision right then to sleep on the floor next to her bed. In the event she got up in the middle of the night again, I would be able to stop her before she left the house.

Because I took care of my mom, I missed **a lot** of school. Children's Services came by our house often. I would make up excuses for why I was not in school because although my mom did not take care of me, she was still my mom - and I wasn't going to leave her. It was her and me against the world! When she was "okay", we would dance and sing, "*It is just me and you against the world. Sometimes I feel it's only me and you against the world. And if one of us is gone, we have God on our side. And if one of is gone, we have God to carry on*". All I had was Jesus, and I thank God: He **never** left my side!

When I hit my teen years, boy did I hit them! I was extremely rebellious and disrespectful. I did not care about anything nor anyone. My best friend and I developed a rap group, and my God-given talent to write songs was being used to vent my frustrations about **EVERYTHING**. The mouth God gave me to sing His praises started cussing people out. That same mouth could drop a sexual innuendo at any given moment.

As my mom's stays in the hospital grew longer, I became even angrier and more vengeful. When I was hurt, I would do whatever it took to get my revenge. I truly lived up to my rap name: Sweet-n-Low. I was 'sweet'...until you messed with me - then I became 'lowdown and dirty'. During that time, I also learned that sex can be used as a weapon. I vowed I would **never** allow another man to have control over me. I would, instead, use what I had to get what I wanted.

Well, **THAT** vow was short-lived. Jesus would not leave me alone. After I got pregnant with my first child, I returned home to the only one who truly loved me: *Jesus*. I saw in my son new life. I understood what it meant to love without expectation of anything in return. That's how I loved my son. I prayed over him and gave him back to God after reading in the Bible that the firstborn belongs to God.

I began developing my one-on-one relationship with God, but I had no one to help me through the healing process. **All** of the pains and secrecies of my childhood were *still* having a negative effect on my life.

With no active father-figure in my life, I began looking for a surrogate father. You guessed correctly if you said, *"Genae found what she was looking for in **BAD BOYS!**"* That was one of **the worst** mistakes in my life. A 'bad boy' without God is a recipe for disaster. I went from spending time with God to hiding on the bathroom floor with my children because I did not want **THAT** man to know I was home.

*For just one day, could I have peace, Lord? No **arguments**. No **beatings**. No **threats**. Just peace, God. **Just peace**...*

My eye-opener came when I had three major losses - one right behind the other. I lost my mom in 2000, my grandmother in 2001, and my daughter in 2004. Those losses left my three sons and me alone. My family had always been small, but it sure got smaller.

There were many days when I did not know whether or not I was going to make it. Depression became my friend. The only reason I did not let it *consume* me at the time was because I wondered who would take care of my children when I was gone.

I threw myself into ministry. *Surely that would help me...*

It didn't.

The effects were still there, except they became even more prevalent. You're probably wondering what the effects of the abuse were.

Here are just a *few* I suffered from:

> ➢ Low self-esteem
> ➢ People-pleasing
> ➢ The inability to say **"No!"**
> ➢ Lack of boundaries
> ➢ Unable to give and receive love
> ➢ Promiscuity
> ➢ Depression

I turned to the church, but (*unfortunately*) they dropped me as well. Instead of embracing and helping me get through the many losses in my life - *beginning with my* **innocence** - they labeled me as a trouble-maker and someone "not good enough for God". I went through a season in which I actually believed them! So, I figured: *If you can't beat them, join them!* I became the good, little Christian who never complained or spoke against any decision the church leaders said. If my pastor said, "*Be here*", I was there. If he said, "*Do not go*", I didn't go.

I went from one type of abuse to another!

Let me pause and digress here for just a moment.

I am an advocate for following the authority God has placed over church leadership, but those in leadership in **my** church played mind games. In its simplest of terms, I was being *spiritually*-abused. The pastor took liberties that were not his to take, all because he knew my brokenness so well. Fear became my constant companion, and because fear cannot operate alone, depression decided to join the party. Depression brought with it thoughts of suicide and feelings of inadequacy.

So, what was I to do? I did not have that answer at the time. I had no one to turn to, so I gave up. Since no one had the spiritual discernment to see that I was hurting, I figured I would not be missed. I tried suicide...again. Just like the first time, God would not let me go - even though that time around, I consumed enough pills to put down a **horse**!

What did I get for my efforts? A very necessary good night of sleep.

However, the pain remained. Enter in guilt. *How could I preach about a loving, forgiving, merciful God to others and not see the same message I preached was for me?* I could pray and intercede for **everyone** else, but found it so hard to pray for myself.

One day, I threw up my hands and said, **"GOD, I CANNOT DO THIS ANYMORE! I NEED YOU TO FIX ME AND FIX ME *NOW!*"** I heard Jesus telling my spirit, *"That's what I was waiting for."*

God was waiting for me to stop looking for what I was missing in mankind, when what I was missing could only be found in **Him**. I began reading the Bible with a different motive. I wasn't just preparing to deliver a message; I was reading the love letter from my Heavenly Father! Every time I saw the word 'love' used in relation to God, I inserted my name in place of the person in the Bible. Doing that revolutionized my life! I came to know God intimately and experienced the love only He can give: **UNCONDITIONAL LOVE.**

The Word of God was healing me. Although I was still in pain (*because it does not go away all at once*), I developed a motto:

"LEAD WHILE YOU BLEED".

I was still hurting (*bleeding*), but I was not going to give up - even when (in the natural) I became the woman with the issue of blood. Let me explain: For **two** years, I was in and out of the hospital because I was losing way too much blood. I was on a constant menstrual cycle (period). During one of my doctor's visits, I was rushed to the hospital. My blood count was so low, if I had not received a blood transfusion right away, I would have been dead.

Because **THAT** issue didn't stop me, Satan came at me yet another way: *REJECTION*.

God had given me a vision for a women's ministry - one that I was extremely excited about. However, not everyone who claims the name of Christ is a *disciple* of Christ. I told a few people about the vision and received more than my share of negativity. I was even told by a pastor that I was to not interact with the women of **his** church because God did not call me. He said, "*Only when God tells me personally [in stereo sound, I suppose] will I release you into ministry.*" I was instructed to continue coming to church, pay my tithes, and prove myself faithful. I was crushed. I even contemplated giving up because it was too much to deal with. Maybe I was wrong… *Was it God I heard?*

Oh, **BUT GOD!** What did **HE** do? He sent me a few people who believed in the vision and, more importantly, believed in the God in me. They prayed me through and supported me, especially during the transition period when I lost my church family, was black-balled in church circles, and was called every name **but** a child of God. Supposedly, God "revealed" to those people that I was a Jezebel, full of pride. I was so tired of the criticism. I felt like Sophia in the movie *The Color Purple*: *"All my life, I had to fight!"* I did not want to fight anymore…

BUT GOD!

God revealed to me that the battle was not mine to fight; it was His - and I allowed Him to fight it for me. I did not do what my flesh wanted me to do. I prayed for (*not about*) those who cursed me. I was free, and *The Word 4 H.E.R.* Ministry was born! Out of my pain, my purpose was birthed. I wanted women to get what I did not have. I wanted them to receive the support of their sisters, affirmation, and hope for their future.

"For I know the plans I have for you" - this is the Lord's declaration - "plans for your welfare, not for disaster, to give you a future and a hope. You will call to Me and come and pray to Me, and I will listen to you"
(Jeremiah 29:11-12, Holman Christian Standard Bible™).

Dr. M.E. Porter - affectionately known as The Soul-Shifter - is a servant leader. She is a preacher who knows how to do business. She is the Pastor and Visionary for The Pink Pulpit Crusade International - a global women's ministry tasked with evangelizing the world. She is a gifted Transformational Speaker and Best-Selling Author. Dr. Porter is the CEO of The Soul INpowerment Group (SIG) - a faith-based coaching and consulting firm - where she serves as Coach, Mentor, and Marketing Strategist. The SIG also houses a publishing house - Soulidified Publishing - where the motto is, "*Publish your soul; not just your words*". Soulidified specializes in Bible Studies, Devotionals, and Affirmational books, as well as transformational testimonies (*taken on a case-by-case basis*). God is her source, and because of that, she ain't worried about a **THANG**!

Ministry Mentions:
I am the Pastor and Visionary of the Pink Pulpit Crusade International - women on a mission to evangelize the world.

I am the Founder of Motivational Outreach Ministers and Mentors - ministry for the masses, outside of the church walls and into the trenches!

Dedications:

To the WOG who stood firmly with me in ministry three years ago when God released me to advance.

To Team ME: You ALL held my arms at times, not even aware you were doing so. You walked through the valley with me and did not retreat!

Social Media:

Facebook: IamMEPorter
Facebook: ThePinkPulpit
Twitter: SoulutionSage
Twitter: ThePinkPulpit
Instagram: SoulutionSage

Web:

www. MarilynEPorter.com
www.ThePinkPulpit.com

He Took My Dead Stuff
By Dr. Marilyn E. Porter

There were many times before today - *this day, November 22, 2016* - that I sat down to write this story, and I struggled so hard! I penned a few other books here and there. I even put a few words together for **other** people's book projects, but I *could not* for the life of me write **this** chapter!

Then, about two weeks ago *(counting back from the aforementioned date)*, I had a life-changing experience. Truth be told, I nearly lost my life - **BUT GOD!** As I found myself in a must-rest-and-relax-situation, I finally realized this: ***The reason I had struggled to write this story was because I had not lived it yet!*** I am not even the same woman I was just two weeks before this date, and this story **must** be told by the woman I am today.

The Comfort of Pain

I do believe it was Bishop T.D. Jakes whom I heard say the following words: *"There is something about a woman that allows her to get in bed with pain and snuggle up with it."* **Lord, have mercy!** Those words have rang in my ears since the very moment I heard them - which was quite a few years ago.

I have checked my own snuggle-factor when it comes to pain, and what I have found is that it's the **emotional** pain that seems to make the best snuggle-buddy. I mean, after all, not many people choose to endure physical pain for any length of time. *That's how Motrin™ and Tylenol™ stay in business!* However, the situations that and people who linger on and are welcomed in (sometimes for months, years, and decades)... it's **that** emotional terror.

As a woman, I will speak from a woman's point of view. I (*as a woman*) have often chosen the very person or people whom I **knew** would cause me pain, yet I was willing to take on the pain-challenge to have a very brief moment of happiness - or what I **thought** would make me happy...at times, choosing a few days of pleasure for the price of years of pain. It just doesn't make good sense, but we do it - and we do it freely. It's not natural to choose pain for no good reason. It is not in the divine design to choose pain simply for the purpose of feeling the pain!

The saddest outcome of the comfort of being in pain is that once our mind and body comes accustomed to the feeling of what was once a source of discomfort, we no longer recognize it as something that could cause permanent damage. We don't realize we are created for all of our parts - body, mind, and spirit - to work together to allow us to live an abundant life. When one or more of those pieces malfunctions, our very destiny is at stake. Prolonged emotional pain - not to be confused with longsuffering, which is specifically designed to help us endure the things that **God** has called us to (*don't get that mixed up with enduring just to endure!*) - is a malfunction in the soul that can transfer into the physical body. That may sound like some New-Age Mumbo-Jumbo, but I assure you it is not. **I just lived it!**

The Physical Manifestation

The event had been planned one year prior, but due to circumstances out of our control, we had to postpone the 2015 event. *Motivation from the Mountaintop* was an extraordinary experience in 2016. God showed Himself in a very special way for me. As the Founder of the organization, it was only befitting that I would be the close-out speaker for the event. My words were simple and easy to digest, yet powerful enough to reach the hearts of the women who were under the sound of my voice.

I was pleased. I **knew** I had poured out exactly what the Holy Spirit had led me to pour. It was a good day. My heart was smiling, my spirit was nourished, and my soul was soaring! My body, however, had not gotten the memo that it was a good day. Just moments after I spoke to the women, my stomach began to hurt. It wasn't a very intense pain, but more of a discomfort that caused me to have to sit down.

*Mind you: I was **used** to pain, so I was not the best judge on the range or depth of pain I was feeling.*

The event concluded and I returned to my hotel room. I was still feeling slightly uncomfortable, but not wanting to be the downer for the other ladies, I pushed myself to go for a brief walk. My stomach pain continued to worsen and *(again)* I needed to take a seat. We made a stop at a Barnes and Noble™ for me to gather myself for a few moments. The hotel was less than 100 feet away, but the **pain** was beginning to scream louder. My body was trying to let me know *something* was wrong - something I would not be able to fix all by myself.

That was on a Saturday afternoon. I endured two more days of acutely uncomfortable pain in Utah before my plane left on Monday afternoon. *Thank God for my dear friend who took heed to my level of pain and suggested we buy a pair of sweatpants for me to ease the discomfort of the denim jeans I was wearing.*

I then deep-breathed my way through a **very** uncomfortable two-and-a-half-hour plane ride to Atlanta - and then a horrible walk through the busiest airport in the United States. Feeling feverish and nauseous, I made my way to my car. Feeling faint at that point, I *still* pushed myself to drive about 40 minutes to a friend's house. As I approached her home, I called her on the phone. She didn't sound like she wanted company, so I made the decision to drive myself four-and-a-half-hours to my daughter's house in Tennessee! I didn't get very far before I had to stop and do something to ease the blood-curdling pain I was in. I was about 50 miles into the trip. I stopped and slept in the travel stop parking lot for a few hours and then made my way on to Tennessee.

I had never been so happy to arrive in my life! I went in the house and headed straight for the shower. I had been traveling since 9:00 a.m. the day before, believing somehow the shower would be relaxing enough to ease my pain. I was wrong! So, I laid on the couch and slept...and slept...all day.

Towards the evening, I began to notice there was a slight bulge that had initially appeared on the left side of my abdomen that Saturday afternoon. It had begun to turn red. *"Hmm... I wonder what this could be?"* I mumbled to myself. I took two 800 mg. Motrin™ - and laid back down. It was in that moment I realized I had not used the bathroom (went "number two") in quite some time. I quickly concluded part of my discomfort **must** have been because I was constipated.

I woke up the next morning - which was *Wednesday* - and my stomach was totally inflamed! I mean, it was red as a Crayola crayon! I made the decision that it was indeed time to visit the doctor (*whom, by the way, I had just seen the day before flying to Utah - the Wednesday of the previous week*). I had been given some new medications for Type II Diabetes and (*in my head*) I believed all of my pain was stemming from an allergic reaction to the medication.

I waited to see the doctor for about 30 minutes because my doctor was booked and could only see me in between her other patients. I saw that as a **super** blessing! When an unfamiliar doctor entered the room, he immediately made the assessment that the swelling and redness had *nothing* to do with an allergic reaction. He then told the nurse to send me to the Emergency Room (ER) and to inform them they should consult the surgical team!

KABOOM!

I won't bore you with the ins and outs of the ER visit, but I **will** tell you that *almost immediately* after being seen, I was admitted. Shortly after being admitted, I was in surgery for three-and-a-half-hours - a surgery that should have taken only one hour! To say that I had been literally hanging in the balance between life and death since I felt that very first pain on the previous Saturday would simply not express the urgency of my medical situation nor what it had been over those five days.

I had **dismissed** the pain, **endured** the pain, **medicated** the pain, and **slept** with a pain that was *killing* me. That was my life's experience with pain. The emotional traumas I had experienced had trained me how to cope with pain that is at **LEVEL 10** as though it was a **LEVEL 2** - and it almost cost me my life.

Why "**KABOOM**"? Well, the onset of that *initial* pain I felt back in Utah and had traveled with for the next four days was an **explosion** in my abdomen. I had a growth *(the doctor called it a hernia)* in my belly the size of a fist that had exploded and ruptured my intestines. Yelp! You guessed it! That bulge in my stomach - the one that made those sweatpants much more comfortable than my jeans - well, that was my intestines spilling out.

I was literally "spilling my guts"!

Talk about walking through the valley of the shadow of death! Death was surely on my heels, but goodness and mercy showed up and carried me on through! **Glory to 'through'!**

The Death Stuff

Most doctors are engrossed in science, which often makes it difficult for them to believe in an unseen Jesus. I got that sense from my doctor, but **God** used his wisdom, skills, and knowledge to fix my very damaged body.

Medically, the explosion had ruptured my intestines - which had stopped the flow of blood...which meant death to anything that did not have blood flow. A portion of my intestine died and had to be removed.

Whew, Jesus! Just thinking about it makes a praise well up inside of me!

When the surgeon entered my room the next morning, these were his very first words: "No worries, Marilyn - because *everything that I removed from your body was already dead anyway.*" **ORGAN MUSIC, PLEASE!** My body could not move, but I'll tell you what: My **SPIRIT** was doing the Holy Dance when he spoke those words! *Thank you, Lord, for removing the dead stuff!*

The doctor didn't stop there, though. He continued with his conversation. "You see, the *blood* supply had been cut off for quite some time, so all of the nerves and tissues were no longer viable." **WHAT?** Lord, this man doesn't realize he was preaching a sermon to me in that hospital! What happens to us - as Christians - when we cut ourselves off from *THE BLOOD* supply? I **KNOW** you are feeling that thing right now...just like I did.

God kept me during a time when I didn't even realize I needed to be kept. I was in death's shadow. I had come from the mountaintop in Utah (**literally**), only to find myself in the valley of a medical emergency - and **HE** kept *ME*! I want you to know that **HE** is a keeper, a life-preserver, and a light that can and will diffuse the shadow that may be cast over you. I **KNOW** it was the hand of God that carried me through those *five days* of my body literally dying and rotting.

You can't make me doubt **HIM**. Don't waste your precious time *ever* trying to!

"Although I may have to walk through the valley of the shadow of death - where unknowingly death may be looming - I will fear NO evil, for YOU, oh Lord, are with ME and I know you have me surrounded on all sides."
Dr. M.E. Porter's Translation of Psalm 23:4

Almena L. Mayes is an Associate Minister at Coley Springs Missionary Baptist Church in Warrenton, North Carolina, a Minister and Presenter for the Pink Pulpit ministry, and the Best-Selling Author of *Just Eat the Beans*. She is currently serving under watch care at Berean Christian Church in Lithonia Georgia. "Mena" (as she is called by family and friends) has degrees in Communication and English. She is also a singer and songwriter who spreads the message that God saves, heals, and restores. She feels a responsibility to present the message of God's never-ending love to all people. Mena states, "We all have issues. We all have problems. By being transparent to ourselves, God, and God's people, we can grow beyond them." She is the mother of three beautiful adults and has three wonderful grandchildren.

Social Media
Facebook: Just Eat the Beans

Email:
JustEatTheBeans@gmail.com

The Conclusion

While You Are in the Valley
By Minister Almena Mayes

They said I may never walk again. I sat there as they told me that Multiple Sclerosis (MS) was going to rob me of my life. I could go on to tell you how difficult it was to deal with this knowledge and how it stole my hope, my marriage, and my faith; however, that is not the tale **God** wants told! Here is the thing: MS sat me down for a while, but it could not keep me down!

BUT GOD!

God's power superseded **everything** the doctors told me. It is not that we will not be visited by suffering, but that we will overcome by the power of an Omnipotent God!

His power is manifested through chastisement.

God's power reaches beyond where we, as natural beings, can comprehend. There are always situations and circumstances that we can't see our way out of. Then, we suddenly find ourselves on the other side - wondering how we got there! Contrary to what most people believe, that is **not** the reward of the *faithful*.

God found me in my backslidden state. I was in a place of sorrow and pain. I was doubting His existence. I was lost and floundering. Yes, I was going through the motions; going to church, going to Bible studies...and going **crazy**! I was spinning out of control! I had no idea that all of that was a set-up. God was preparing me to proclaim His glory and attest to His power.

My story is only important as a vehicle of revelation. God picked me up from my lowest point and brought me to my highest. It seems cliché to some to say, *"Picked me up, turned me around, placed my feet on solid ground"* - but that is **exactly** what God did.

What I learned from that experience is that we have to learn to look at what some perceive to be a curse as a *blessing*. The power of God does many things for us. Sometimes, however, we fail to realize it until an issue arises in our lives. Those issues help to grow our faith, build our testimony, and strengthen our endurance. In doing those things, God has an opportunity to be glorified. We have to look at the positives in those situations.

For example, in my backsliding, God's power brought me back to the right path. Just as a parent disciplines his child, God uses **His** authority to do the same thing. His love mandates that He brings us home to Him by any means necessary; even if that means He has to chastise us to do so. Through His chastisement, we realize that He is all-powerful and, regardless of the scenario we have created with our choices, **His** plan for our life does not change. **His** desires for us will be fulfilled. We must complete our assignment.

His power is manifested through change.

There is no way an individual can come into contact with the power of God and remain unchanged. Acknowledgement of God's control is the first step towards spiritual growth. As a child of God, we come to understand that we need God's power more than we need anything else.

Let's look at a couple of common situations:

> We can be hungry - *starving even* - and have no money nor means to buy food. Then, unexpectedly, we receive a check in the mail! This is not a **new** thing. *Didn't God send the children of Israel manna from Heaven?* The money buys us food, but **God** recognized our need and His power supplied it!

> You are in a car accident. Everyone says there is no way you should have walked away from it unhurt, but you have no broken bones and no internal injuries - **nothing** that will cause you pain. God's power protected you from a situation designed to take your life. *Didn't He do the same for Daniel in the lion's den?* Something that should have killed him served to bring God glory. **God's** power put a hedge of protection around Daniel...and you.

Situations like those leave us changed. When we experience God's power on such a personal level, we can **never** be the same. The way we think, feel, and talk about God is directly affected by the touch of His hand and the exposure to His power. We are irrevocably changed!

God's power is manifested in our daily walk.

Walking with God daily is very important. He desires an intimate connection with us. Being grounded in His Word and His will is mandatory for Him to manifest His power in our lives.

I have been fortunate enough to see His power demonstrated in my life time and time again! He pulled me out of relationships, closed doors that I should have never opened, and guided me in directions that have been beneficial to my growth. I have come to the understanding that God's power is a gift that is activated in my life through faith, dedication, and diligence. I am a living testimony to His power here on Earth. He is the source of my strength, and it is by His grace that I can be all He has called, destined, and ordained me to be. It has nothing to do with me nor anything I have ever done or failed to do. It has nothing to do with my efforts - or lack thereof. **God gets all the glory!**

When we realize all things are done through and for God, we have truly experienced spiritual growth. This pleases God. He wants to develop us in a way that will allow us to use the power He has stored within us. We don't have to wait until we feel we have become "perfect" to allow God to use us. We can begin moving in Him as soon as we feel Him moving *within* us.

As we passionately pursue a relationship with God, He stirs up the gifts He has placed in us. Taking time to talk to God is invaluable. Those little, private chats are the times that build intimacy.

Think about the quiet times you spend with your spouse or significant other. Those are the times when you share your secrets, your hopes, and your dreams. Those are the times you get to know one another. *Those are the times you strengthen your relationship.*

The same is true when it comes to your relationship with God. Those quiet times spent with God are when He gives you the power to exercise your spiritual gifts. We possess so much of God within us. Sometimes, He has to shake us up for us to come to that realization. God creates opportunities for us to pray diligently when we need a work done, to worship without ceasing - knowing that He hears us, to praise when we can't see the breakthrough, and to walk in authority when it seems all is lost. Every one of those situations results in the manifestation of God's power that lies inside of us.

God's power is manifested in our lives.

"Yea, tho I walk through the valley of the shadow of death, I will fear no evil" (Psalm 23:4).

Translation: "I AIN'T SCARED OF Y'ALL!"

God's power makes us bold! We can begin to face all challenges with a spirit of victory. When you know that you know, the outcome of **every** situation you walk, talk, and think is different. *How confident can you be when you know the game is rigged, the deck is stacked in your favor, and the fix is in?* God already told us He has given us power and authority over **all** things on Earth. He also tells us that **no** weapon formed against us shall prosper. That means there is nothing in the natural and nothing in the spiritual that can defeat us. They can't take us out because we have already been recognized as the winners!

Winners don't make excuses: They expect solutions! God desires us to walk in expectation. Faith says all things are possible through Christ. If that is the case, then we should expect all things! The **power** of God compels us to focus on Him, knowing that He has it all in control.

Winners are comfortable being uncomfortable. God never said it would be easy to wield the power He has bestowed upon us. Growth requires that we step out of our comfort zones. Why? Because growth means the space you are in will become too small!

Winners expect to exceed expectations. We tend to put limits on God by thinking He can only do what is *humanly* possible. God's power is **omnipotent**! He can do things the human mind cannot begin to fathom. He doesn't just meet the standards; He performs exceptionally! He expects the same from us. We don't just do the bare minimum. His power within us allows us to be able to perform miracles in His name!

Winners are focused. God desires that we keep our eyes and minds on Him and His ways. To get things done, we have to *focus*. Sometimes, the assignment God gives us seems impossible. God gives us the steps to complete each assignment. By staying connected to Him, we know how to move, where to move, and what to move to complete every challenge.

Finally, winners don't dwell on past mistakes. We make mistakes just like everyone else does. What makes us different is that we don't *dwell* on them. God does not expect perfection: He expects **commitment**. Don't allow a fall to hinder your progress or diminish your power. Instead, take the lesson and move forward.

The power of God touches every aspect of life. When we recognize that, we understand **WE ARE MORE THAN CONQUERORS!**

Contact:

SoulidifyME@gmail.com

Follow us on Facebook!

Soulidified-Publishing-LLC

Made in the USA
Las Vegas, NV
07 April 2022

46987650R00039